RUNNING FOR BEGINNERS

The Most Complete Guide to Learning to Run, Mastering the Proper Form, and Boosting your Performance

Matt Jordan

©**Copyright 2017 by Matt Jordan- All rights reserved.**

This document is presented with the desire to provide reliable, quality information about the topic in question and the facts discussed within. This Book is sold under the assumption that neither the author nor the publisher should be asked to provide the services discussed within. If any discussion, professional or legal, is otherwise required a proper professional should be consulted.

This Declaration was held acceptable and equally approved by the Committee of Publishers and Associations as well as the American Bar Association.

The reproduction, duplication or transmission of any of the included information is considered illegal whether done in print or electronically. Creating a recorded copy or a secondary copy of this work is also prohibited unless the action of doing so is first cleared through the Publisher and condoned in writing. All rights reserved.

Any information contained in the following pages is considered accurate and truthful and that any liability through inattention or by any use or misuse of the topics discussed within falls solely on the reader. There are no cases in which the Publisher of this work can be held responsible or be asked to provide reparations for any loss of monetary gain or other damages which may be caused by following the presented information in any way shape or form.

The following information is presented purely for informative purposes and is therefore considered universal. The information presented within is done so without a contract or any other type of assurance as to its quality or validity.

TABLE OF CONTENTS

INTRODUCTION 1

WHY RUN? 2

ARE YOU FIT TO BE A RUNNER? 6

CHOOSING THE RIGHT GEAR 9

BEFORE YOU LACE YOUR RUNNING SHOES 21

WALK TO RUN 23

GETTING STARTED 27

STARTING TO RUN 45

NUTRITION AND HYDRATION 58

THE UNCOMFORTABLE SIDE OF RUNNING 62

KEEPING THE MOTIVATION ALIVE 66

CONCLUSION 68

PREVIEW OF "MARATHON RUNNING BY MATT JORDAN" 69

INTRODUCTION

If you have ever started running just to find yourself unlacing your shoes a couple of minutes later, welcome to the club. Every experienced runner, I included, has gone through that not-made-for-running phase.

But people cannot be divided into those who can run and those that are simply not made to pound the sidewalks. Everyone can achieve the endurance to become a marathon runner. The trick is to know how to embark the running journey the right way.

Luckily for you, this is the best starting-off point. Reading this book will equip you with all the right information and throw a couple of tricks up your sleeve for when the training becomes harder.

From why and how you should run to teaching you the ultimate technique to boosting your running performance and becoming the athlete you've always wanted to be, this book is the only running guide you will ever need.

Having the answers to all the questions that the new runners have, as well as clearing up the confusions and misconceptions that go hand-in-hand with running, this is the only guide that has the power to push the couch potatoes to enter the world of fitness.

Are you one of those that need a get-up-and-go? If so, click the 'buy' button and join me on this fitness ride.

WHY RUN?

Many people think of running as a pointless endeavor. You spend your time and energy just to get back to the same spot where you started from. Others think of running as boring and unproductive. I know a couple of them who have nothing against playing a soccer match and running across the field. They have a goal – to catch the ball and score. To them, running around the block is meaningless. Why anyone would want to do that, they wonder.

It's true that it can hurt; it is also true that it requires effort and willpower, and yet, millions of people all over the world do it on a regular basis.

I really cannot give you the answer to why people run. Everyone has their own reasons. Why do we do most of the things we do? Why do we paint? Or ski? Or play video games?

Some run because they are passionate about it. Others like to push themselves. Other people run because they enjoy the ecstatic sensation of setting a new record. Logic cannot be really found on the running's side.

And while I cannot tell you why your neighbor goes out for a jog at five in the morning, I do know why you should start running and how you can benefit from pounding the roads.

Running can drag many, many benefits into your life that goes way beyond the obvious of stripping the extra pounds away.

Running Helps You Lose Weight

Let's start with the most obvious reason. Being the most effective way of burning calories, running has become the best weight-loss tool for those who want to melt off the stubborn fat around their bellies. Do you know that a 160-pound person can burn over 850 calories with one hour of running?

Running Extends the Lifespan

It is not only Chinese herbal remedies that have the power to increase the longevity of life; running can help you stay young too. Among the main benefits that running brings is that it keeps us young on the inside while keeping diseases away and supporting our muscle tone and strength.

Running Prevents Diabetes

Hitting the ground running can help you keep the sugar levels in your blood in check by burning the excess glucose levels and keeping your blood clean. That is the most powerful weapon against some serious, life-threatening diseases such as diabetes.

Running Decreases the Stress Levels

There is no better tool for flushing the stress away than going out for a run. This physical activity can build up a balanced emotional health and promotes mental clarity. That is why people who struggle with mental and mood disorders are advised to follow a regular running routine.

Running Keep the Heart Healthy

Although at this point it may seem so, but running isn't an exercise that robs you of your free time and hurts your legs. It is an activity that elevates the blood flow and the heart rate which contributes to the heart arteries to move more vigorously. This lowers the blood pressure, makes your heart more 'elastic' and closes the door to strokes and other cardiovascular diseases.

Running Increases the Lung Capacity

When you run, your lungs work hard. The harder they work, the more efficient they get. That will not only prevent you from developing breathing problems as you grow older, but it will also restore your lung health if you used to be a smoker.

Running Strengthens the Bones

There is no friendlier exercise to your bones than running. Running increases the density of the bones and significantly lowers the risk of developing osteoporosis later in life.

But what about beyond the health benefits? What other aspect of your life can benefit from you measuring the trails?

It Gives You Your 'Me' Time

Runners know that this exercise is best for clearing the head. And who doesn't need that in this fast-paced world? Had a cramped day? Pressure at work? Spent hours stuck in traffic? Put on your running shoes, pop your headphones on and enjoy being alone with yourself.

It Can Help You Make New Friends

Running is definitely one of the best and easiest ways to make new friends. The best part? You don't have to be afraid of sounding weird since you will meet health-conscious people who share the same goal and inspiration.

Great News for Your Furry Buddy

If you're tired of playing catch-the-stick with your dog, then take him out for a double run. That way you both will benefit from the activity, plus, it will be super fun.

It Can Save You Money

Running doesn't require special sign-ups or costly fees. The only thing you need in order to stay fit and healthy are the right clothing and footwear. Oh, and your motivation, of course.

ARE YOU FIT TO BE A RUNNER?

Running is a task that puts pressure on the body, and it is somewhat physically demanding. That being said, not everyone can put on the athletic wear and go and run a marathon.

You cannot possibly expect to be able to run 3 miles if you spend your free time as a couch potato. Almost everyone can be a runner, but not everyone is ready to adopt running as a lifestyle choice straight away. This modern society tends to encourage the neglect of the musculoskeletal system which makes the inactive ones, great candidates for running injuries.

The first thing you need to do before even thinking about buying a new pair of running shoes is to take a look at your medical history. Do you suffer from any health conditions that can affect your running? Are you overweight? Are you underweight? Do you have a heart problem? High blood pressure or Diabetes?

The best way to see if you are competent to hit the trails is to pay your doctor a visit. He will measure your blood pressure, assess your weight and height, and will give you advice accordingly.

Remember, if you are overweight and want to take advantage of running and melt the excess fat away, you will probably have to hold on to that thought for a while. If you do not exercise regularly and are obese, chances are, by taking a run you will only do yourself more harm than good.

The extra pounds you are carrying around put a high pressure on your joints which is why it will be extremely hard for you to run. What you need to do is to slowly increase your daily activities and balance your diet. Your doctor will probably advise you to start with walks that will help you get fitter and eventually enable you to participate in faster and longer runs.

But what if you are not overweight nor have any other health problems? How can you know whether you are fit to run or not? Well, there are three key points that can send you to the running track: flexibility, stamina, and strength. Let's take a quick test and see where you stand with these:

Your Flexibility

Lie on the floor with your legs straight, wrap a towel around your left thigh, and hold both ends of the towel with your left hand. With the help of the towel, try to lift your left leg (still keeping it straight) toward your chest. Make sure that the right leg and your hips don't move. Is it possible for you to reach a 90-degree angle with your left leg?

If No - If you cannot reach 90 degrees doesn't mean that you cannot run, just that you are not flexible enough. To increase your flexibility, make sure to practice that exercise daily, trying to hold your legs in that position for at least 20 seconds.

Your Stamina

Walk 2 miles at your normal speed. How long did it take you? Did you do it in 32 minutes or less?

If No – You are not ready to run yet. Start by walking 15 to 20 minutes a day to improve your physical activity. When you feel ready for taking the little steps, try our walk/run technique.

Your Strength

Try to hold a plank (which is the part of the push-up when your body is up) for three sets of thirty seconds. Also, try to do 10 pushups and 10 squats. Can you do all that?

If No – Know that having strong legs, core and arms are the essential for running. Before you start with the running plan in this book, try to strengthen your muscles a little bit.

CHOOSING THE RIGHT GEAR

What's there to choose? Put on your shorts and your only pair of running shoes that's been collecting dust on your shoe rack since college, and visit the nearest park, right?

Well, yes if you're into spending the next few days limping around. Those running shoes and jogging bottoms you see in the sports stores are not sold to make you the fanciest, best-looking runner in the park. They are actually essential for providing you with comfort, ensuring safety and improving your running performance.

But how do you pick the right running equipment? Should you just go into the store and ask if they have those cute Nikes from the shop window in your size? It is not so simple actually. There is a whole lot to take into consideration before you head to the register. Here is what you should know before going shopping for your very first running gear.

FOOTWEAR

Shoes are the runner's biggest asset (besides the great physical condition, of course). When times were simpler, so were shoes. You could just buy canvas sneakers and hit the pavements running. So, what has changed? Do the shoe companies promote the fancy running equipment just to maximize their profit?

Actually, no. People have made a lot of discoveries since a couple of decades ago, and the fact that bad running shoes are the main culprit for running, injuries is one of them. Of course, there is no magical pair of sneakers that will make you the world's greatest runner, but choosing the one that fits your feet perfectly is the best health insurance. And I am not just talking about getting the size right.

There is one very important thing you should know of before hitting the store, and it is called *pronation*.

Running, obviously, forces your feet to undertake some extremely complex and dynamic movements. When making these forceful movements, your feet strike the ground with the outside of the heels. First, they roll downward and inward as they touch the ground, and finally, the heels lift and the feet's balls push themselves off the ground.

The degree in which your feet roll inward when they meet the ground is called pronation. But not everyone pronates the way they should. Some people tend to supinate.

Supination is just the opposite of pronation, and it happens when the feet roll outward when they strike the ground, not inward. So, before you point your finger to what you think are the best running shoes in the store, make sure to determine your running style and see whether you are a pronator or a supinator.

The Wet Test

The wet test is the easiest way of finding out your degree of pronation. And it's quite simple. Have a piece of white paper laid out on your bath floor the next time you take a shower.

If your tiles are dark and you can clearly see your footprints, there is no need for the paper. While your feet are still wet, leave a footprint on the paper (bathmat also works well). Analyze the shape of the footprint. The print can have one of these three shapes:

It can be arched. If your footprint is curved and emphasizes an arch by mostly showing the heel and the ball of the foot, that means that you are a supinator. Supinator are less flexible runners. Their bone structure is somewhat rigid, and their feet cannot absorb the striking shock well.

It can be normal. A normal footprint still has a curve, but it also shows the entire foot. That means that you are normal pronator. Normal pronators are neutral runners. They have the lowest risk of injury.

It can be flat. If your foot makes a full contact with the ground and your print shows no arch, which means that you tend to over-pronate. The over-pronators have a really low instep, and when they experience injuries, it is usually their calf muscles that suffer.

Your old shoes can also show you your degree of pronation. Just grab a pair and check the shoe line. Does the heel shows wear at the inner edge or the outer edge?

The Shoe Construction

Your running shoes will be your new best friend, and therefore, it is important to know their anatomy. Besides, if you don't know how the shoe is constructed, you may never find the right fit.

The Last – The shoe last is the sole of the shoe, the underside. The last of the shoe is probably the most important factor that needs to be considered.

There are three types of shoes: straight-lasted, curve-lasted and semi curve-lasted. You can easily check the type of the shoe by just looking at the underside.

Just imagine that there is a straight line that runs down the middle of the shoe. If the imaginary line divides the shoe into two equal halves, then the shoe is straight-lasted.

If the line is really curved, then it is a curved lasted shoe. The semi curve last has a visible, but slight curve at the top.

The three types of lasts correspond to the three types of feet. If you over-pronate and have a flat foot, then the straight-lasted shoes are the perfect choice. They will offer you a supportive and rigid base that will control your feet's tendency to over-pronate.

If your feet are inclined to roll outward, and you are a supinator, you need shoes with good cushioning that will offer your feet flexibility. The curve-lasted shoes will do just that. They will support your feet and force them to roll inward which will help them to better absorb the shock of striking the ground.

Those of you who are neutral runners, you are in luck because you really don't need to be seeking special cushioning or extra-rigid base. Semi-curved shoes are the perfect choice for your normal feet.

Upper – Upper is the fabric part of the shoe where the laces are. This part protects the sides and the upper part of the feet from the toes to the heels. The design and the fabric of the upper don't really affect the running process, so you are free to choose according to your own preferences.

Midsole – This is the rubber part that is between the last and the upper part. The midsole is in charge of controlling the movements of the feet and preventing, where possible, the inclination of overpronation or supination.

This cushioning material is usually made from gel, foam, plastic, and some of the major manufacturers also use air pockets (Think Nike Air Max) in order to reduce the weight of the shoe and increase performance.

Inner Sole – The inner soles can be easily removed or replaced. They are found on the inside of the shoe and provide extra cushioning and support.

Heel Counter – The heel counter is what holds the back of our feet. They are mostly made from cardboard and plastic and are there to hold our feet firmly and prevent them from going up and down.

Toe Box – The toe box is also very important. Just like the feet, our toes are also not of the same size. When buying shoes, it is extremely important to inspect the toe box well and see if your toes can be moved from the inside, or not. The best way to do that is to place your index finger inside the shoe and see if it can fit between the front of the shoe and your longest finger.

A Match Made in Heaven

The best advice that I can give you is to visit a specialty running store in order to receive the most professional service. The people who work there are trained to offer you the best choice that matches your foot type and will do a much better job than if you decide to go measuring lasts on your own.

Most running shoes will serve you perfectly for about 400-500 miles, and that is the only 'critical' buy that you'll have to make.

Keep in mind: If you plan on running a race or a marathon in the near future, it is best to buy two pairs of shoes. One that you will be using for your training, and one that will be new for the marathon. Your training shoes can get easily worn out and will most likely decrease your performance on the big day.

These are the general tips when it comes to buying running shoes:

Your feet will most likely swell during running, so it is best to try on shoes in the late afternoon because at that time our feet to a degree are the largest.

It is common for people to have different-sized feet, so it is best to have the salesperson measure both your feet first.

Wear socks. It is recommended to wear running socks when trying on shoes. If you don't have any, it is probably wise to buy a pair before you buy your shoes.

Try both of the shoes and go for a run-up and down the store. Okay, you don't actually have to make a circular jog, and it may seem weird, but it is really highly advised for you to get a feel if the shoes will fit your running activity or not. Most decent stores will have a running machine for you to try this anyway.

The heel must be firmly pressed against the heel counter and not be able to slide up and down.

Your running shoes should be half to a full size larger than your ordinary shoes.

In a perfect world, you should be able to find the perfect shoe match in the first store you enter. However, that is not that likely to happen. Many people struggle to find the best running shoes. If you are one of them, wait before giving up on your dream to run a marathon. If the stores don't offer what your feet are looking for, try *orthotics*. Orthotics are inner soles that are custom-built to fit your unique preferences. These can be either hard or soft and made from different materials. The orthotics are inserted inside the shoe fix the specific faults of the shoe and offer your foot a great support that will improve its performance.

CLOTHING

No one says that you actually have to have special clothes designed for running to go out jogging. However, if you are serious about running and being healthy, and want to improve your performance while staying safe, then choosing the right clothes to wear can make a huge difference.

First of all, when it comes to running clothes, keep in mind that it is quality that matters. You don't have to buy 5 running bras. It is a far better option to have one specially designed and wash it every day, than it is to have quantity that lacks quality.

The running clothing items, just like any other clothes really, are mostly determined by the weather outside. If it's how you dress less. If it's not, extra layers are the best. You must be thinking, okay, but what to wear? The more important question is what not to wear. And I have a single answer to that question – cotton. That new cotton shirt may be great for going out for a drink, but if you wear it for running, it will keep you in bed for days. Yes, cotton clothes make you catch a cold easily. How? Cotton doesn't dry that easily. When it gets wet, it stays wet for many hours. You don't go out wearing wet clothes, do you? The same way you shouldn't run with wet clothes. That will not only make your running experience super uncomfortable, but it is also dangerous.

Now, let's get back to 'what to wear' question. Like I said, depending on the weather, you can wear clothing items designed for running: shirts, tights, shorts, pants, bras, jackets and vests. When the weather is warm, your running clothes should protect you from the heat and keep you cool. When the weather is cold, the running clothes will keep you warm, but ensure that you will not be hot, since you will get warm up once you start running and sweating.

When looking to buy running clothes, there are a couple of factors that you have to consider:

- *Quick Drying* – The perfect running clothes must be able to soak up the sweat quickly, keep you dry and protected from catching a cold.
- *Moisture Wicking* – The fabric that is moisture-wicking takes the perspiration away from the skin quickly and keeps you dry.
- *Thumbholes* – Many running clothes with long sleeve have thumb holes that will keep your hands warm. You can skip the gloves if your thumbhole-jacket covers your hands completely.
- *Sun Protection* – Always choose clothing items with high UPF ratings that will protect you from the UVA and UVB sun rays.
- *Compression* – Running clothes with compression provide a cozy fit and keep you comfortable.
- *Inner Liner* - When buying shorts, it is recommended to buy those that come with an inner liner that can act as underwear and decrease resistance.
- *Mesh Vents* – Buy tops with mesh panels only. That can keep your sides, underarms, back and other body areas that are easily heated, cool.

The Fabric

The fabric of your running clothes is not only important but crucial. Before buying the pants based on the design, check the label and see if it is made of 'technical' clothing. Technical fabric is lightweight, breathable, anti-itching and most importantly, will keep your skin dry:

- *Merino Wool* - Besides that, it contains all of the previously mentioned features, merino wool is also antimicrobial which will keep the odor away. It is the best fabric for regulating the body temperature, meaning that it will keep you cool when it is warm and will make sure you are warm when the temperature drops.
- *Polyester* – Polyester is great at keeping the moisture away from your skin which will improve your running performance.
- *Nylon* – Whether used alone or blended with other quick-drying fabrics, nylon is a great moisture-wicking fabric that is extremely durable.

<u>IMPORTANT:</u> Have you ever wondered why running shoes and clothes have such bright and vivid colors? It is to keep you safe on the road. Running in the middle of the day isn't always an option. Sometimes, when the days get shorter, or your schedule doesn't allow it, you will find yourself striking the ground at night. You have to stay a moment in those moments. Bright vests and jackets and clothes with reflective strips will make sure that you will be seen even when the streets are not well-lit.

OTHER EQUIPMENT

You don't really have to spend half your paycheck on fancy gadgets to be a great runner. And while running equipment other than the right pair of shoes and comfortable and breathable clothes may not be essential, there are some gadgets that your running can indeed benefit from:

- *Heart Monitor* – If your doctor thinks that it may be wise for you to track your heart rate, then heart monitor is something you should always have with you when you are out running. It is an amazing advice that will tell you when it is time to slow down, even if your legs don't want to listen. This is great for those who tend to over train and need an alarming sound to make them stop.

- *Sunglasses* – Don't let the blistering red sun send you home earlier and put a stop to your morning routine. But peering your way through shouldn't be an option either. Make sure that you have a nice pair of running shoes with you when running. You don't have to purchase a high-tech pair that will hurt your heart if you leave them on a bench somewhere. However, make sure that the sunglasses you choose will offer you a 100% ultraviolet protection.

- *Watch* – What better way to see how long you have been running for than the old-fashion wrist check? The trail isn't exactly the place for your Rolex, but purchasing a cheap running watch that has all of the features you need will be a great investment.

- *Cool Towels* – Buy a cool towel, get it dry and snap it a few times and you have the perfect relief from the high summer temperatures. These towels won't get you icy cold but are just the thing that can cool you down when the sun begins burning your skin.

- *A Flip Belt* - If your clothes don't have any pockets then a Flip Belt is the Perfect storage solution. The Flip Belt is a belt where you can store your ID, keys, and phone. You can lock everything in, by simply flipping the belt over.

- *Yaktrax* – Who says that you have to hit the gym when it is snowy outside? Who says that the treadmill is the only option when the roads are snowy and icy? Just like you put those chains on a car's wheels, the same way you put the yaktrax on your running shoes. Yaktrax are super convenient, easily attachable and will give you a great grip that will keep you from falling on your bottom.

BEFORE YOU LACE YOUR RUNNING SHOES

Running is one of those things that everyone wants to be good at, but most people don't know how. Be honest and answer this. Have you ever tried to run just to give up 5 minutes afterward? I know a couple of them who had bought the most expensive running equipment and gave up the dream of running the very next day. Is it the lack of determination the problem? Or is running just so damn boring? What is it that makes people dread the thought of spending their mornings jogging?

If you want to be a runner but don't want to fall for one of the many traps this modern world will most likely throw your way, then read on to see how not to fail at running.

Time, Not Miles. The very first reason why people fail is because they get easily disappointed. They set the bar too high, and when they cannot get to their desired finish line, they throw their running shoes out the window. Don't start your running journey running in miles, but in minutes. It is much more productive to try to run 15 minutes than it is to run 3 miles. Don't measure the distance, but try to increase the time you run, a little bit every day.

Have a Goal. No matter how small, having a goal to accomplish is the best motivational gauge. For instance, let's say that your goal is to be able to run 5 miles without stopping. Obviously, you cannot do that after 2 days of being a runner newbie. The best way is to try to break that 5-mile goal into other smaller goals. To become able to run 5 miles, you will need improved fitness and a much better physical condition. So, you may want to make eating well, exercising and running for x minutes every day, your sub-goals.

Keep a Diary. Keeping a log and making it easier for yourself to view your running progress is the perfect tool to keep yourself motivated. Being able to see how your performance advances every day will keep you on the right track and give you the drive to do even better.

Find a Friend. Although running is considered to be a solitary sport, quitting usually comes easier for those beginners who undergo this challenging task alone. Instead, why not find a friend who is fitness-conscious and invite him/her to start this journey together? That way you can keep each other motivated and besides, it is much more fun.

Take Your Rest. Rest days are just as important as training days. It is your time to recharge your batteries and load yourself with some more energy that can increase your running performance. Pushing yourself too hard will not only exhaust you, but it can also injure you. Don't be drastic, but patient. If you want it bad, you can run a marathon. If it was possible for Oprah, it is possible for you too.

WALK TO RUN

Most of us can easily walk for a couple of miles before the fatigue kicks in. Walking is natural to us as we are designed so we can do it efficiently for a couple of hours. Running, on the other hand, puts us under a higher amount of pressure, simply because it requires more work. In order for you to run, you have to lift your feet and body off the ground, and then land back on it. And you have to do it over and over again. That means that throughout the process of running, your body will consistently be receiving the shock of landing. For those who are not in a decent physical condition, this process will result in fatigue, pains, muscle aches, or even some more serious injuries.

But just because you have been a couch potato your whole life doesn't mean that you have to injure yourself to become a fit runner. There is a safe method that allows beginners to improve their shape so they can start running the right way and keep those injuries at bay. That is the walk/run method.

The walk/run method, as the name suggests, is a combination of running and walking. It is perfect for the newbie runners who want to decrease the fatigue and become able to run without having to stop to take a break every 15 seconds. And while it may seem to you like something designed for a third-grader when it comes to beginning a run, the walk/run technique can really make all the difference:

- It can be a great motivation booster in the beginning, which is extremely important

- It can help you gain control over the fatigue and exhaustion which can be of great help later on because it can prevent you from injuries

- It can train you to endure long runs and finish your races

- Do you know that many experienced runners also combine walking and running? They say that it relieves the pressure on their muscles which is great for ditching injuries as well as the mileage endurance.

Now that we have made it clear that the walk/run method will not embarrass you once you blend between the experienced runners in the park, let's see how you can actually start this training.

First of all, know that running is nothing like learning how to ride a bike. You cannot just master it in one day. You will need to slowly build up your condition and pace, and that will take some time. Or 8 weeks to be precise. I strongly suggest you run the walk/run style for 8 full weeks before you begin setting higher goals and start pushing yourself. And here is how you can get started:

- **Warm Yourself Up.** Before you start pounding, you need to warm yourself up with a 5-minute walk first. Never start running the second you leave your house. Instead, warm up the muscles with a short walk first.

- **Get the Starting Ratio Right.** This is a very simple method; the only thing you need to do is to get the 1:6 ratio right the first week. That means that after 1 minute of jogging, you should walk for 6 minutes. For instance, if you decide that you can run for 3 minutes, then you should walk for 18 before starting to run again.

- **Walk Before You Get Tired.** The biggest mistake that inexperienced runners do is that they run until they lose their breath completely. Once you exhaust yourself, it will take a lot longer for your muscles to recover and chances are, you will give up on running. By slowing down and switching to a walk before you get too tired, your muscles will recover quickly, and you can cover more distance and time.

- **Walk the Right Way.** Walk slowly, but do it with a strong and short stride. Make sure not to do it leisurely, but keep your arms pumped so that you can keep your raised heart rate so you can easily transition back to running.

- **Gradually Increase.** As the time passes, you should gradually decrease your walking time and increase the time you jog.

If you want to build up your condition and become able to run for 30 minutes continuously, then this 8-week walk/run plan will help you achieve just that:

- *Week 1* – Start walking for five minutes to warm up. Jog for one minute, then return to walking and walk for 6 minutes. Repeat this three times. It is recommended to run for three sessions this first week.

- *Week 2* – Warm yourself by walking for five minutes. Run for 2 minutes, then walk for five. Repeat this four times. Do three running sessions this week.

- *Week 3* – Again, start by walking for 5 minutes. Switch to running and jog for 4 minutes and slow down by walking for 2. Repeat this four times. Do four sessions of running this week.

- *Week 4* – After walking for five minutes, run for 5 and walk for 2 minutes. Repeat this 4 times. This session should be done three times this week.

- *Week 5* – After warming up, run for 8 minutes and walk for two. Repeat this four times. Do three session this week.

- *Week 6* – Warm up, jog for nine minutes and walk for two. Repeat this three times and also do three sessions of running this week.

- *Week 7* – Walk for one minute and jog for 11. Repeat for three times and do three weekly running sessions.

- *Week 8* – Try by walking for five minutes, run for 20 and end the workout by walking for five minutes again. Increase the running time each day, so that by the end of this week you can run for 30 minutes continuously.

After this, you will be able to run 30 minutes non-stop without exhausting yourself. You should do it three times a week.

GETTING STARTED

Those of you who think that running is simple are not that far from the truth. You can indeed simply put on your running shoes, pop in your headphones and hit the road. It can be as simple as that. However, when you are still not familiar with both the good and bad things that can happen as a result of you striking the pavements, you might want to hold on to that extra energy and make sure that you are fully prepared for this challenging process first.

To put you on the right track, this chapter will explain everything that you need to know before you begin with your long non-stop runs. From where to start running to how to cool down after a good run, let this chapter be the guide that will enable the achievement of your running goals.

WHERE TO RUN?

Yes, you can run anywhere, whether it is the pavement in your neighborhood, the sand on the beach, or that hill up the mountain. Your feet will strike the same, whatever ground you choose to put underneath them. So what's all the fuss with picking the right surface? While your feet may be fine with landing on both hard and soft surfaces, your body is somewhat pickier. The evenness of the surface also matters a lot, and in many situations, it is the main culprit why injuries swoop in. The pressure that your body receives when the feet strike an uneven ground indicates the chances for injuries. But, is there one best surface that will be your body's best friend and increase your running performance? Many say that there isn't, however, when you are just starting to run, I would say that an ideal surface for you would be a forest ground that is cushioned with pine needles. But since only a few of us actually have the privilege of having this ideal surface nearby, the rest of us must work with what the surroundings offer.

Experts say that the key to success is in variety, meaning that choosing to mix up the ground you run on is the key to your healthy performance. Of course, I don't mean to mix them up literally, but simply to avoid running on a single trail every day.

Each running surface comes with a list of pros and cons, and in order to determine when to hit which of these trails, you need to learn about how and when your body can benefit from them.

Grass. If there is no forest nearby, there is no need for you to sprinkle pine needles on the road in order to avoid injuries, grass will do just fine. Grass also has a low impact on the body and is therefore recommended for beginners. I can understand why the pavement may seem like a more convenient option for you, but keep in mind that this is the best surface to avoid injuries at this initial stage. Many studies have concluded that grass is the surface that is the friendliest to our bodies because it lowers the pressure on the muscles, tissue, and bones.

But grass can be tricky. Know that running in the park can be somewhat stressful due to all the distractions such as dogs and walkers. Besides, you have to be more careful when running on grass and watch out for those hidden holes and rocks that may cause another kind of injury.

Dirt. Dirt roads are rated the second best surface for running because of their combination of hardness and flexibility, which can be great for those runners who have suffered an impact-related injury in the past.

However, just like grass surfaces, dirt can also be uneven, so watch your steps to avoid hurting your ankles.

Sand. Sand seems great simply because it is soft and the risk of suffering an impact-related injury is small. A run on the beach can also be more relaxing, not only because of the environment but also because of the low pressure that this surface has on the muscles.

But sand isn't as great as it seems. The softness of the sand makes it a pretty unstable surface which screams ankle injury. Running on sand requires a lot of strength since it is hard to get a good grip. For beginners, it is recommended to avoid these sand-related accidents. If you, however, particularly love running on the beach, then do it on wet sand because it is a much secure surface.

Asphalt. If your goal is to train for a race, then at some point (usually after 'mastering' the grass), your feet must meet the asphalt in order to prepare yourself, since most races happen on the street. Asphalt lowers the tension on the heel, and it has shown to be a pretty great running surface, as well.

Keep in mind that running on the streets is not safe. Make sure that you wear bright colors with reflective strips that will keep you noticed. Also, lose the headphones so you can increase your awareness and reduce the danger.

Concrete. Those of you who live in big cities will find running on sidewalks to be the safest and most convenient option. However, it is also the worst one. Know that concrete is one of the hardest surfaces and can, therefore, increases the stress in your joints and muscles. Although good shoes with proper cushioning can help, try to limit the running time you spend on the sidewalks.

Treadmill. First of all, know that running the same distance on treadmill and on a real surface is not the same. Treadmills also pull you as you run, which makes the whole process easier and allows you to run a long distance. Running that same mileage on asphalt or grass will be trickier.

Now, the treadmill as a running surface is great if you have suffered an injury or want to reduce the stress on the muscles. However, not being able to observe the surroundings as you pass them by can be boring and quite discouraging.

Hills. Although the climbs are really determined by the area itself, beginners should try to avoid running up and down hills and climbs when possible. Running up a hill requires a great physical condition and running strength, which you, at this initial stage, lack. Running down a hill may look like a better choice as it can increase the pace. However, that is only short-term, since the downward slopes put too much stress on the joints.

So, which one to choose? Start with grass, avoid the hills where possible, and then mix the other surfaces in. Having a running route is great, but running on the same surface all the time, not so much.

WARM-UP TECHNIQUES

"But, I am not training for a marathon." It doesn't matter if you run to prepare yourself for the upcoming marathon, if you do it out of recreation or you use running as your stress-relieving tool. Warming up before starting to run is essential if you want to keep up a good shape and prevent injuries.

The biggest mistake that beginners make when running is that they skip the warming part altogether, thinking that it is a useless waste of energy that could maybe cover an additional mile. This is not only wrong but absurd. Warm-up techniques are there to prepare your legs and muscles to endure the long distance, not to soak up the energy and contribute to exhaustion.

And while we said how walking before running is a great way to warm up the tissue and prepare your legs for the run, it is simply not enough. Sure, the walk/run technique doesn't actually require any particular strength or preparation, but if you want to make running an important addition to your lifestyle, then making sure you'll maintain your fitness and top performance is crucial.

Make sure to set aside 10 minutes for warming yourself up before pounding the ground. That will wake up your central nervous system, increase the temperature of your body, raise your heart and breathing rate, and prepare your whole body for the running exertion.

Won't a simple stretch do? It is important to mention that for many years warming up and stretching were interchangeably used terms. Now that we know better, we not only know that they mean two different things, but we also know that basic and static 30-second stretching is quite the opposite from beneficial, since it has been linked to injuries.

Dynamic stretching, on the other hand, loosens up the muscles and improves the leg movement:

Toe Walk. This simple exercise will develop strength around your ankles, and it will activate the shin, calf, as well as your feet muscles.

- Stand with a straight spine and your shoulders back at hip-width apart.
- Lift your heels off the ground, keeping the balance on the balls.
- Step forward with your right foot, while extending onto your toes.
- Balance yourself while swinging the left arm.
- Repeat with your left feet and right hand and continue to walk that way.

Heel Walk. This exercise will reduce the heel tightness, as well as activate the muscles in the lower part of your leg and ankles.

- Take the same posture as the exercise before. Straight and with your legs at hip-width apart.
- Lift your toes off the ground, keeping the balance on your heels.
- Step forward with the right foot, while keeping your toes pointed upwards.
- Balance yourself while swinging the left arm.
- Repeat with your right foot and continue to walk on your heels.

Inchworm Walk. This is a somewhat more challenging exercise that can mobilize not only your leg muscles but also your shoulders and lower back.

- Take a press-up position, meaning that your hands should be on the floor and under your shoulders, your arms and spine straight, feet at hip-width apart and your balance kept on the toes.
- Now, try to walk your feet towards your hands, which means that your body should be folded at the hips.
- Hold that position, then slowly walk your feet back to the initial press-up step. Repeat.

Straight Knee Walk. This will activate your calf muscles, as well as mobilize your body.

- Stand straight and keep your legs apart at hip width.
- Stretch your left arm in front of you, parallel to the floor.
- Lift your right leg and bring it closer to you. Ideally, your leg should touch your left arm, but if you cannot do that, just lift it as high as you can.
- Hold this position briefly, then step with the right leg.
- Repeat with the other side and continue walking this way.

Hip Exercise. The mobility of your hips is essential for a proper running performance. This exercise will open up your hips and make them more flexible.

- Stand straight with your feet apart at hip width.
- Lift your right leg. With your left hand, grasp the right leg at the ankle. Grasp the knee with your right hand.
- Slowly lift your leg towards your chest.
- Hold that position, then release and repeat with the other side.

Scorpion Stretch. This exercise is perfect for mobilizing the mid-section and improving your body's flexibility, which is essential for a proper performance.

- Lie on the floor (preferably on a mat) with your face down.
- Stretch your arms to make a 90-degree angle with your body and keep the palms down on the floor.
- Slowly, raise your right hip off the floor.
- Now, gently bring your right foot over your back as if you are trying to reach your left hand. Your back should be twisted, and the right knee bent.
- Hold this position briefly.
- Repeat with the other side.

Spiderman. This exercise works both of your legs and improves your hip flexibility, as well.

- Take a knee press-up position, meaning that your knees should be on the ground and your hands too.
- Place your right foot next to the outside of your left hand, keeping the knee bent at 90 degrees and leveled with your armpit.
- Now, reach forward with your left hand, and step forward and stretch the left foot.
- Repeat with the other side.

Superman. This simple exercise will increase your running performance and endurance by increasing stability in your knees, ankles, and hips.

- Stand straight and keep your feet at hip-width apart.
- Stretch your right hand in front of you, parallel to the floor. The palm should be faced down.

- Raise the right leg off the floor hind you and stretch it until it becomes parallel with the floor.
- Bend your upper body and your left knee for stability.
- Stretch your right arm farther more.
- Hold this position briefly.
- Repeat on the other side.

Repeat these exercises for 10 minutes, and you are good to go.

COOL-DOWN TECHNIQUES

Just like warming up, cooling your muscles down after a run is just as important. By doing it the right way, you can prevent soreness, injury, as well as gradually decrease your elevated heart rate. And while basic and static stretches can help you cool down (not warm up like people used to think), there are also some other more muscle-oriented techniques that will help you congratulate yourself properly for completing a challenging workout.

Downward Dog. This stretch will strengthen your calf muscles and core and may prevent Achilles tendon injuries.

- Place your knees and hands on the floor, keeping your back parallel to the floor and your knees right below your hips.
- Lift the knees and lower your heels.
- Push your hips upward, so your body is in a V shape.
- Hold this position briefly then return to the first step.
- Repeat.

Adductor Stretch. This exercise works the adductor muscles of the hips and thighs.

- Stand straight and keep your feet apart at hip width.
- Bend your left leg so that the knee will come over your left foot.
- Your right leg should be extended.
- Repeat on the other side.

Side-Lying Rotation. This stretch will relax the front of your body from the running stress.

- Lie on your back with your hand on a folded towel and keep your arms by your sides.
- Place a foam roller on your right side, bend your left knee and place it on the roller.
- Bend your right leg also and allow it to turn in the rotation direction.
- You can extend the stretch by reaching your left arm in the opposite direction (behind you).
- Return to the first step and repeat on the other side.

Hip Flexor Stretch. This simple exercise can prevent pelvic imbalances.

- Kneel on your left knee with your toes tucked under.
- Place your right foot in front of you, keeping the right knee at a 90-degree angle.
- Place your hands on the hips.
- Lean forward and place the weight on your right leg, bending the knee over your right foot.
- Hold briefly then repeat on the other side.

Brettzel. This exercise is great for improving the thoracic mobility.

- Lie on your right side and support your head on a folded towel.
- Pull your left knee towards your chest and hold it with your right hand.
- Reach your right foot back so you can grasp it with your left hand.
- Hold briefly, return to the start and repeat on the other side.

Hamstring Stretch. This simple stretch will loosen up your hamstrings after a workout and prevent injuries.

- Lie on your back on the floor keeping the legs straight and your arms by your sides.
- Lift your right leg keeping your toes parallel with your body.
- Grasp it with your hands and pull it back gently to slightly extend the stretch.
- Return to the first step and repeat on the other side.

THE PERFECT FORM

Running is not just going one foot in front of the other. In order to project the maximum energy with the least pressure, you have to learn to take the right posture and running form.

When thinking about the right way to run, people mostly focus on the feet and their movements. But you would be surprised to know that even though running is performed with the feet, they actually play only a small part of what we call a great running form. Whether your feet will meet the ground the right way or they will strain your muscles, believe it or not, depends on your entire body.

Here is a detailed info on how to take the perfect form, reduce the muscle stress and boost your condition. Don't feel overwhelmed if you cannot execute all of these pointers. They are not there to teach you how to run, but how to run better. Only with regular practice you can adopt each of them and start your training the right way.

Head. Your head plays a key role in the way you run, and its alignment is crucial for your performance. When running, your head should be held high and the gaze directed straight in front of you. Avoid looking at your feet to keep your neck, head, as well as your spine straight and aligned for the proper form. Make sure not to jut out your chin, too.

Shoulders. Keep your shoulders loose and low. They should be square and kept in level. As your running progresses and you become more tired, you will notice that your shoulders will most likely rise up. When that happens, simply shake them out to relax them. Try not to swing them around from side to side too much.

Arms. The movement of your arms is the key factor of running. By moving your arms, you receive the drive to push yourself forward, as well as push yourself faster. Your arms are best kept at a 90-degree angle and moved in the rhythm of the legs. They must swing, just remember not to swing them across your body. Keep the swinging forwards and backwards, but close to your body.

Torso. You must keep yourself tall and straight at all times. Of course, I don't mean to run like a robot; it is natural for you to lean forward slightly. However, make sure that you do not hunch over or lean backwards. Keeping your shoulders in the right position and relaxed should be enough for your torso to be held in the right position. Just remember not to twist it from side to side, but run with your chest tall to allow the full lung capacity.

Hands. You should never run with clenched fists. Instead, keep your hands relaxed and well-structured. Your fingers should touch slightly. If you hold them tensed and clenched, that tension will get transferred to the rest of your body and will burden your heart. Just, imagine that you are holding a potato chip and you don't want to break it to ensure that your hands will not be tensed.

Hips. The hips are probably the easiest to position the right way because it is simple. If you hold your shoulders and torso straight, then the hips will have no other choice but to follow and join the perfect alignment. Make sure that they are faced straight ahead and not leaned forward because that will ruin your whole form.

Legs. When learning to run the proper way, it is natural for beginners to sort of lengthen their stride and lift the knees higher so they can run faster. However, the long-distance and experienced runners know that keeping the knees low and the strides short is much more productive because that way the energy can be preserved. Instead, they increase the turnover of their feet. You should make sure that your feet will land underneath your knees, not in front of you. That will keep the strides short and the impact on the knees minimized.

Ankles. Although it may seem like they don't move, your ankles should actually roll inwards when running. This will allow you push yourself forward properly. If your ankles are too stiff, try some more dynamic stretched to loosen the calf muscles.

Feet. Make sure not to thump with each impact. Instead, land gently and lightly. You should land between the midpoint and the heel, and roll your feet forwards when taking off. Your feet shouldn't land flat or noisy. Running is supposed to be light and quiet.

BREATHING PROPERLY

Breathing is one of the biggest obstacles when it comes to running efficiently. Almost every beginner have struggled with shortness of breath. Ask any experienced runner, and you will get the same answer – when they first started, they also experienced the loud huffing and puffing.

We are trained to breathe from our chest. After all, we do that every second of every day. But that is simply not enough to provide all our muscles with the necessary amount of oxygen when running. That's when side stitches and aches come in.

The way we regulate the breathing while running is crucial for our energy and can, in fact, have a deep impact on the whole performance. If you want to be a better runner and run a long mileage, you cannot do that without the proper breathing method.

Breathe From the Belly. Try not to breathe from the chest but from the diaphragm, or as we like to call it, from the belly. Make sure that your belly moves up and down with each breath you take.

Breathe Deeply. Your lungs are small, and they cannot provide you with enough air to pack all of the muscles while running on their own. That's where deep breathing comes in handy. Deep breathing helps you drag more oxygen into your body. When we breathe deeply, the diaphragm is pressed, which causes the lungs, as well as the abdomen to expand and to fill our lungs with more oxygen. Deep breathing is crucial when running because it prevents nausea and fatigue.

Find Your Breathing Pattern. It is really helpful to try to coordinate the breaths you take with your steps. If this seems like an impossible thing to do, then you are probably running too fast. Slow down in order to match your steps with the breathing. If you are running at a medium pace, try to inhale deeply and hold the breath for a three or four steps. Then, exhale for the same number of steps. For an intense run, the breathing will also increase to follow the tempo. When running intensely, a breath for every two steps you take seems just about right.

Mouth or Nose? Go for a quick online search on proper breathing techniques for runners, and you will find yourself confused in front of the contradicting advice. Some say breathe through your nose; others claim that the mouth will help you inhale more oxygen. But which one is better? How can you know which breathing method is better? Well, here is the answer. Breathing through your nostrils allows you to inhale a small amount of air that, unfortunately, is not enough to satisfy the large need for oxygen that your muscles require. Think about blowing a balloon with your nose. That is how efficient nose breathing can be while breathing.

That brings us to breathing through the mouth. It is true that the inhaling through the mouth will allow a more substantial oxygen flow through your body. However, there are a lot of things that are not right about breathing through the mouth while running. The most important of all is that when the temperatures drop, breathing through the mouth can have a negative impact on your running performance. We all know that the cool air is dry, and breathing through the mouth will only provide you with asthma-like symptoms such as wheezing, which your lungs will not like. These symptoms can significantly decrease your energy and ruin your performance.

So, what should you do? The best approach is to train both mouth and nose breathing, and more importantly, to learn how to do it at the same time. That will significantly increase the air flow and will supply you with enough oxygen to keep your muscles worked up. For chili weather you can put something over your mouth (like a bandana), that will help you to keep the humidity by trapping the moisture from your breath.

Practice Breathing. Just like you practice and to exercise to strengthen your muscles so you can improve your performance, the same way you can train to strengthen your lungs and breathe better:

Sit and put your hand on your belly. Take a deep breath and count to 4 each time you exhale or inhale. Check with your hand to see if your belly is moving. If it is not, that means that you are not breathing deeply enough.

Go swimming. If you have difficulty in matching your steps with your deep breaths, then perhaps swimming can help. Besides that, it is also a great exercise for your muscles that will contribute for you to become a better runner, swimming also puts an emphasis on proper breathing, which is yet another way that your performance can benefit from.

Put Down Your Cigarette. It probably goes without a saying, but smokers don't make great runners. Smoking can seriously wreck your process of running by damaging your lungs.

STARTING TO RUN

Running three times a week will bring many beginners the fit body and the perfect physical shape that they have dreamed of. However, if your goal is to become a serious runner, to be able to run faster, farther, or even to enter a marathon, then there is a certain training that you need to go through in order to achieve your goals.

TYPES OF TRAINING

Here are some training types that you can gradually start implementing into your running routine after you master your walk runs:

Easy Run

Easy or recovery run is a run that is performed at a pace that is much slower than your normal pace. These runs are usually done after an injury or after a hard workout, for instance after a race. These simple and easy runs are not there to increase the weekly mileage of the runner without taking any of the performance.

Easy runs can also help your body recover after a stressful run. These runs shouldn't put any effort on your body but must be done slowly. Most experienced runners love going out for easy runs because of the enjoyment they bring.

Slow and Steady

In the beginning, all of your runs should be slow and steady. This type of running is great for improving your condition and boosting your endurance. But what exactly is slow and steady? Slow and steady runs are those runs when you are comfortable with your pace. Imagine that you are out running with your friend and at the same time having a conversation. If you feel like you can go for a long time before becoming tired, then you are slow and steady running.

Slow and steady runs are great for learning pacing. They will keep you from going too fast, which is the biggest mistake that beginner runners make. This is also the best run to practice breathing and match it with your steps. By keeping the same pace throughout the whole run, you will also be able to analyze your style and be able to detect potential injuries in time.

After your walk/run routine, the slow and steady runs are highly recommended. Once you learn how to comfortably run 30 minutes a day, three times a week, you can then start gradually increasing the time or the distance of your slow and steady runs. After that, you can safely proceed with more challenging runs.

The Long Runs

The long run is, perhaps, the most important part of your beginner's training routine. It is building up your distance and slowly getting closer to your goal. These long runs last long enough to make you moderately to severely tired, and the distance or the time of the run depends solely on your unique condition and your endurance only.

The long run should be incorporated to give you confidence that you can actually achieve something more than simply jogging in the park, and that your performance will not be something that will leave you behind during races. For instance, if your goal is to run a 5k race, then the long runs should mean that you should include one 5k run a week for a couple of weeks before the actual event. This will boost your confidence and motivation. However, note that these runs do not apply for the marathon, as running the whole mileage for a couple of weeks can actually exhaust you and will most likely have a reversed effect on your performance on the marathon day.

I highly suggest you include one long run in your weekly training schedule. This run should be at least 25% of your weekly mileage.

Progression Run

Progression run is the type of run that is started with your normal pace and ended with race or marathon-pace. These runs are more challenging and therefore are not recommended in the first few weeks of the beginner's training schedule. Once you start running 30 minutes a day effortlessly, you can then think about increasing the speed of your runs.

Speeding up means that you will have to drain more energy and to be able to run progressively and at the same time efficiently, you will need to be in a pretty good shape first.

You don't have to be particularly interested in marathons or races to choose to take this type of training. Progression run can be beneficial on many other levels. It can train your body to run on lower oxygen levels, your lung's capacity will be increased, as well as your body's ability to use the energy reserves properly.

Fartlek

Before you can actually become able to go out for a progression run, you have to slowly start introducing fartlek to your training routine. Fartlek is basically a speed play, meaning that you add a few sprints in your normal, steady run. Think of fartlek as those small 'race you do to that stop sign' type of races we loved as kids. This is very similar to that. You run with your steady pace, you pick a final destination (whether a tree, a bench or a stop sign), you sprint to that point, and then you transit back to your normal pace.

The fartlek intervals are small, usually around 200 meters.

Up and Down the Hills

Like I said earlier, hills require a lot of work and should be avoided in the first couple of weeks. However, if you are serious about boosting your performance, then introducing hills to your running routine will be more than beneficial.

Once you become aware of your good physical shape and know just how much you can endure, then you can safely start to climb up and down hills. Running on hills can seriously improve your endurance since this will strengthen your leg muscles, boost your cardiovascular performance, and not to mention, it will help you burn more calories.

The trick is to run at steady pace until the hill, then to sprint up as fast as you can, and then to slowly walk back down to recover from the shock.

BOOSTING YOUR PERFORMANCE

Most people think that in order to improve your running performance, the only thing you need to do is run more and more each day. However, that is far from the truth. It may seem strange to you now, but to become an experienced and long-distance runner, your running training has only one part in achieving that. There are other training exercises that go hand in hand with running. Without these exercises, you will never have the strength to endure the physical challenge and the stress that the process of running puts on your muscles.

Core Training

The core is essential for keeping your body in perfect shape and being able to run efficiently. Your core consists of your spine, as well as the muscles of your back, abdomen, and hips. The muscles are in charge of providing a proper base for the arms and legs. Therefore, you can only imagine how important the core for your running performance is. A strong core means more power and endurance in such a dynamics sports as running.

Lower Body Roll. This core exercise will strengthen the core muscles and improve your hip mobility.

- Lie on the floor with your feet together and your hands above your head.
- Bend your left leg, so the knee becomes leveled with the hip.
- Reach that leg across the body while rotating the hips in the same direction until you roll over.
- Now, extend your right leg diagonally across your body while keeping your upper body on the floor until your leg doesn't force it to roll.
- Repeat on the other side.

Bird Dog. This core exercise will mostly strengthen your lumbar spine.

- Kneel down on all fours with your knees below the hips and spine in a neutral position.
- Raise your right arm in front of you with the palm down. Extend the left leg and raise it until it's parallel with the floor.
- Hold briefly, return to the first step and repeat on the other side.

Sprinter Crunch. This super popular exercise will improve your running posture.

- Lie on the floor keeping your arms at your sides, and your legs stretched.
- Turn your palms toward your body.
- Lift your shoulders off the ground, bend your left knee and bring it closer to your chest.
- Bend the right arm and bring your elbow close to touch your knee.
- Hold briefly, return to the first position and repeat with the other side.

Stability Ball Crunch. Another great exercise for keeping the abdomen contracted.

- Sit on a stability ball and walk your feet in front of you to form a 90-degree angle.
- Place your hands behind your head.
- Crunch your abs while lifting your shoulders and pushing the back lower into the ball.
- Return to the starting position and repeat.

Medicine Ball Slam. This powerful exercise will work your shoulders and strengthen your core.

- Hold a medicine ball with your hands and stand with your feet at hip-width apart.
- Lift your heels off the ground, support yourself on your toes and raise the ball above your head.
- Drive the ball down in one movement, using the force of your core.
- Drop the ball and bend your knees to pick it up.
- Repeat.

Resistance Training

Just like core training, resistance training is also crucial for the progress of your running training. During a resistance training your muscles work against the resistance, which can only increase their strength and make them more 'endurable.' This resistance training is the perfect exercise for toning the most important muscles for running.

Calf Raise. A perfect exercise for strengthening the calf muscles.

- Stand with your feet apart at your hip width and your heels over the edge of a low step.
- Your toes should be pointed in front of you, and your arms should hang at your sides.
- Raise your heels to be standing on the balls of your feet only.
- Return to the first position and repeat.

Push-Up. This simple and popular exercise is actually one of the most effective for strengthening the shoulders, arms, and chest.

- Lie with your face down on the ground.
- Tuck your toes under and place your hands a little bit wider than your shoulders.
- Lower the body gently until the upper body slightly touches the floor.
- Push your body from the elbows to get it back into the starting position.
- Repeat.

Kettlebell Swing. This simple resistance exercise will work the muscles of your glutes.

- Stand with your hip wider than your hips.
- Lift the kettlebell with a deadlift to let it hang loosely.
- Bend the knees and lean your body forward from your hips.
- Push yourself forward with the hips to stand straight, that way that the kettlebell becomes swinging upward and forward.
- Drop your hips when it swings back, lean your body forward to lower it.

Single Leg Squat. This exercise is successful at strengthening a couple of muscle groups in the legs.

- Stand with your feet apart at hip width and extend your arms in front of you.
- Bend your left knee and lift your foot behind you. Make sure to stabilize the spine by engaging the core.
- Bend the right knee and bend your body at a 45-degree angle.

- Bend your left knee and lift the foot behind you.
- Now, reverse this movement and repeat the exercise on the other side.

Walking Lunge with Dumbbells. The dumbbells will increase your resistance and strengthen your leg muscles.

- Take a good posture and stand with your feet apart at hip width.
- Keep your arms by your sides, holding a dumbbell in each hand.
- Bending at your knees, hips, and ankles, take a step with your right foot.
- Drop your body down and make sure that both your knees are at 90-degree angles.
- Hold this position briefly, lift yourself up, and step forward with the left foot.
- Repeat on the other side.

YOUR TRAINING SCHEDULE

If you still haven't got a clue on where to start and how to incorporate these training types into your running routine in order to train yourself to run farther and faster, then hopefully, these next schedules will point you towards the right direction.

The Initial Training Schedule

After you master the walk/run technique and become able to run 30 minutes, a day, then it is time to top your performance with some more challenging types of training. Here is a simple weekly training program that can boost your endurance in the first few weeks after the initial walk to run method. You can follow this program for as long as it takes for your body to prepare for more demanding activities.

DAY	ACTIVITY
Monday	Easy run
Tuesday	Steady run combined with a 10-minute fartlek
Wednesday	Rest day
Thursday	Steady runs combined with hill climbing
Friday	Core and resistance training
Saturday	Rest day
Sunday	A long run

Increasing the Mileage

Once you get ready for longer and more demanding runs, you can start increasing your mileage. This is a basic foundation program about how you can go from 6 to 22 miles a week.

	Mon	Tue	Wed	Thu	Fri	Sat	Sun	Total mileage
Week 1	2 miles	C and R Training	2 miles	Rest	C and R Training	2 miles	Rest	6 miles
Week 2	C and R Training	Rest	2 miles	2 miles	C and R Training	3 miles	Rest	7 miles
Week 3	3 Miles	C and R Training	Rest	2 miles	C and R Training	4 miles	Rest	9 miles
Week 4	C and R Training	4 miles	3 miles	C and R Training	Rest	4 miles	Rest	11 miles
Week 5	4 miles	C and R Training	Rest	5 miles	C and R Training	5 miles	Rest	14 miles
Week 6	C and R Training	4 miles	4 miles	C and R Training	Rest	6 miles	2 miles	16 miles
Week 7	3 miles	C and R Training	5 miles	C and R Training	Rest	8 miles	3 miles	19 miles
Week 8	C and R Training	5 miles	4 miles	C and R Training	Rest	10 miles	3 miles	22 miles

If you start this program and see that you still cannot execute the mileage, don't get disappointed. Simply repeat the first four weeks for 2 or three times, and then, start the program again.

Every second week (which means week 2, week 4, week 6 and week 8), you can substitute one core and resistance training with exercises like cycling and swimming for about 30 minutes. Your core and resistance training should last 20 minutes in the beginning, and then they should be gradually increased to 30 or sometimes 40 minutes.

NUTRITION AND HYDRATION

It is understandable that when you embark the running journey, your body will become hungrier for fuel. That is why it is of crucial importance for every runner to adapt a healthy lifestyle that consists of a healthy nutrition and proper hydration. But what exactly is healthy and proper, and how much do runners actually need? Since there are many diet misconceptions wrapped around the process of running, I have decided to devote a chapter of this book to that matter, and explain it thoroughly so you can really grasp why and how much is the balanced diet important for your overall running performance.

Nutrition

Nutrition is essential for every aspect of our lives but is especially crucial for dynamic sports because it is the main source of energy. And to make sure that your body will operate the proper way, it needs to be 'greased' with the right type of fuel.

Do you know that with every mile you run you burn about 100 calories? That means that your body will start craving an energy refill sooner than normally. The number of calories (source of energy) you have to consume depends on the intensity of your training, of course. You have to keep in mind that for every 5 miles you run, you will burn approximately 500 calories, so you need to be properly 'filled' to ensure proper performance avoid exhaustion and dizziness.

There are some basic nutrition guidelines. However, that can apply to all runners:

Complex Carbohydrates. Try to limit the consumption of simple and fast-releasing carbs that get easily broken down into glucose. Instead, focus on the complex carbs that can provide your body with steady and slow fuel. This includes whole grains, whole bread, whole past, green and starchy vegetables, legumes, etc.

Protein. Protein is the key nutrient for runners because it is crucial for your muscles. The more and farther you run, the more repair your muscles need. And protein is in charge for tendon and repair of your muscles. The best sources of protein are: lean meat (lean beef, chicken breasts, lamb, and turkey), eggs, fish, nuts, and tofu.

Fats. Only the good stuff, of course. Monounsaturated fats will pack you with some amazing properties that your running performance can benefit from. Choose olive oil, avocados, flax seed and canola oil to boost your good fats.

Vitamins and Minerals. Your endurance depends on the vitamins and minerals you consume. There is no need for vitamin or mineral supplements if you consume a balanced diet rich in healthy whole foods. Here are the most important vitamins and minerals for the runner:

- _Calcium_ regulates the muscle contraction and is in charge of keeping the bones strong, so it is essential for every runner. Good sources are milk, leafy greens, cheese, yogurt, tofu, fish bones, soybeans, etc.

- _Zinc_ is in charge of making new enzymes and cell, as well as the process of fats and carbs. Good sources are meat, wheat germ, milk, shellfish, etc.

- _Iron_ is essential for the production of the red blood cells, which are extremely important for the runners since they carry the oxygen throughout the body. Good sources are liver, red meat, leafy greens, dried apricots, etc.

- *Vitamin C* in charge of keeping the cells healthy. Good sources are oranges, goji berries, strawberries, Brussel sprouts, black currants, etc.
- *Vitamin D* keeps the bones healthy. Good sources are eggs, dairy, etc.
- *Folic acid* keeps the central nervous system healthy. Sources: broccoli, liver, citrus fruits, asparagus, peas, etc.
- *Potassium* keeps the fluids in the body balanced. Good sources are bananas, potatoes, chicken, shellfish, fish, nuts, seeds, etc.
- *Vitamin E* protects the cell membranes. Good sources are wheat germ, leafy greens, cereals, etc.

This is what the breakdown for your daily meals should look like:

60 – 70 % of your calories should be carbohydrates
20 – 30 % of your calories should be fats
10 – 15 % of your calories should be protein

PRE-TRAINING

It is recommended to eat the main meal 2-4 hours before the running training so that the food can be digested by the time you hit the pavements. Also, it is a great idea to grab an energizing snack about 30 minutes before the workout. The best choice would, of course, be an energetic snack, such as a slice of whole wheat bread topped with peanut butter and banana slices.

POST-TRAINING

After your workout, your body will be begging you to make up for the loss of energy. The best and quickest way is to simply drink the calories. Aim to drink a recovery drink that has the 3:1 ratio of carbs to protein. Treating yourself with a delicious protein shake after your run is probably the best choice.

Hydration

Almost two-thirds of the human body is made of water. You can only imagine how important water is to our overall health. But for those that sweat a lot such as runners, water is especially crucial.

If you do not consume enough water, your body becomes dehydrated, and the running performance will, obviously, weaken. It is essential to drink plenty of water at regular intervals and the best way to ensure that you will stay hydrated throughout the day is to always have a bottle of water nearby as a reminder.

The best indicator that will tell you whether you are hydrated is your urine. The brighter the color, the more hydrated you are.

But how to stay hydrated during a run? Well, you cannot exactly measure how much water your body will need, but to make sure that the fatigue will stay at bay, it is recommended to drink about 500 ml to 1 liter of water between 60-90 minutes before you start running. If it is not hot outside and you are sure that you are fully hydrated, you don't have to carry a water bottle with you. Otherwise, take your water bottle with you and have about three small sips every 10 minutes.

THE UNCOMFORTABLE SIDE OF RUNNING

Running is a very dynamic sport that puts a repetitive pressure on your body. That is great for your physical condition, your fitness, the shape of your body, as well as your overall wellness. However, most runners will tell you that there is a small price to pay for receiving all of these benefits.

Once you begin with your running program, chances are you will experience some of the discomforts of running sooner rather than later. But don't feel frustrated, since most of them are nothing to worry about. Plus they can be easily prevented with a decent preparation.

- <u>Blisters.</u> These fluid-filled blisters can be very painful and even get infected if you don't treat them. To prevent them, wear socks made of double layers and apply petroleum jelly to vulnerable areas such as the heel.

- <u>Runner's Nipple.</u> If you wear loose-fitting shirts for running, the repetitive chaffing may cause you irritation and bleeding around on or both nipples. To prevent this, wear running clothes. You can also apply petroleum jelly for prevention.

- <u>Runner's Toe.</u> This is caused by the bleeding that occurs under the toenail as a result of wearing unsupported shoes. Make sure to try your running shoes in the afternoon when your feet are swollen.

- <u>Chest Pain.</u> This is very common among beginners who set unrealistic goals for themselves. Build up your running program gradually and move to a more challenging training when you are really ready.

- <u>Cramps.</u> Cramps happen as a result of over-contracting the muscles. TO prevent this from happening, try some massage techniques (later in this chapter).

- <u>DOMS.</u> The delayed onset of muscle soreness happens when a person is not that physically prepared for the training. That is why the warm-up and cool-down exercises are essential.

RUNNING INJURIES

No matter how experienced you are, running injuries are a by-product of the pressure placed on the body by this dynamic physical activity. That being said, it is important for you to be familiar with the most common injuries that the runners suffer from, so you can detect their symptoms in time, take the right treatment and avoid complications.

- Lower Back Pain. This is very common and can happen due to many factors such as improper form, worn-out shoes, uneven surfaces, etc. You will most likely feel stiffness in the lower back that spreads to your thigh and gets worse when you start running. The best thing is to stop the training for a couple of days until the inflammation reduces. If the pain doesn't go away or becomes more severe, contact your physician.

- Muscle Strain or Muscle Tear. The muscle strain or tear is caused by a strong and sudden contraction (like a sudden change of speed). Your muscles will get red, swollen and you will most likely feel twinges of pain. If such a thing happens, stop your training and seek medical advice.

- Bursitis. Bursae are the fluid-filled sacks that serve as 'cushions' between the bones and tendons. Repetitive friction can cause inflammation and will result in a painful condition called bursitis. You can detect this injury by knowing the symptoms of tenderness and pain around the bursa's area. If you experience this, stop your training and contact your physician.

- Runner's Knee. The runner's knee happens when the tendons are tight, or muscles are too weak. It results in a strong pain at the front of the knee that gets worse when walking up and down the stairs or pressing the kneecap. There may also be swelling. The best solution is to rest, hold an icy compress and elevate your leg. If that doesn't help and the knee still hurts after 10 days, contact your doctor.

- Shin Splints. Shin splints usually happen when you start running without warming up your muscles. The symptoms are a dull pain on the inner side of the shin that increases when exercising. This is usually not dangerous and can be easily treated with a bag of ice cubes and rest, but if the pain doesn't go away after 2 weeks, you should seek medical advice.

- Achilles Tendinopathy. This characterizes with swelling of the Achilles tendon and pain, and it happens as a result of putting too much stress on the leg. The only thing you can do is to stop your training and seek medical help.

- Knee Ligament Injury. When a sudden twisting movement occurs, one of the four knee ligaments can be easily ruptured or sprained. The symptoms are pain and swelling around the knee. If you detect these symptoms, it is recommended that you don't try to treat it yourself but seek immediate medical help.

- Iliotibial Band Syndrome. The ITB (Iliotibial Band) is a structure that is much like tendon and is found from the pelvis to just below the knee. Repeatedly bending of the knee can sometimes result in overuse of the ITB and cause an inflammation known as the ITB syndrome. The first symptom is a pain on the outside of the knee. Swelling and tenderness can also occur. Seek medical attention and do not leave your leg untreated.

KEEPING THE MOTIVATION ALIVE

Living at this fast modern pace when the distractions seem to lurk from every corner, you need a strong willpower to keep your running shoes on. Here are some tips that can help you keep that motivational spark alive that will inspire you to go out for a run regularly.

Visualize. The best way to work hard toward achieving a goal is to visualize the results. If your goal is to run a marathon, just imagine yourself doing it. Picture yourself enduring such a demanding and challenging task and having the physical condition to complete it. That will keep you motivated to train and even increase the mileage as your performance progresses.

Be Realistic. Always set realistic goals for yourself to avoid disappointment. No one has gone from a couch potato to a marathon runner, and neither will you. Make sure to gradually increase the time and distance and be realistic about how much you can actually endure.

Reward Yourself. Like a kid that awaits a sweet treat when he does something good, that way you can treat yourself for making a progress. Try to add rewards next to each goal. For instance, if I manage to run 5k this week, I will buy those fancy running shoes I saw the other day. Again, stay realistic and avoid getting yourself disappointed.

Go Exploring. People usually give up on running because after a while it becomes a boring endeavor. Make sure this will not happen to you. To avoid getting fed-up of the surroundings, make sure to change your running route. Go to new and unfamiliar places where running can be just like exploring.

Listen to Music. Good music can fuel your body and give you the energy to run. Make a special running playlist of all the tracks that you think can distract you from thinking about making a break when running.

Register for a Race. Finally, registering for a race seems to be the best motivational gauge, especially it you are competitive by nature. Knowing that you have an obligation to train to become able to endure a race will keep your mind off of the exhaustion and give you the strength to go another minute, another mile.

CONCLUSION

Now that you know how to get off the couch and start running, it is time to hit the stores and gear yourself up. Remember to follow the guidelines that this book offered and you will be ready to sign up for a race in no time.

I cannot exactly promise you that you will be the next Usain Bolt. However, I can guarantee that if you choose to take advantage of this book, you will have no problem in running a marathon in the near future.

PREVIEW OF "MARATHON RUNNING BY MATT JORDAN"

A BEGINNERS' GUIDE ON PREPARING TO RUN YOUR FIRST MARATHON

A Brief History of Marathons

At the start of the 5th century BC, in the town of Marathon in Greece, a battle took place between the Athenians and the Persians. In spite of being hopelessly outnumbered, the Athenians defeated the invading Persian army.

Legend has it that Pheidippides, who was reputed to be the fastest runner in the Athenian army, was then asked to make the 26-mile run from Marathon to Athens to deliver news of the victory. He ran the whole distance without stopping and collapsed into the Assembly shouting "We have won!"

When the Olympic Games were revived at the end of the 19th century, the organisers wanted a popular event that would reflect the heroic origins of the ancient Greek Olympics. The legend of the marathon seemed ideal, and at the 1896 Olympic Games, the first competitive marathon was run from Marathon to Athens. The distance was 25 miles, and it was won by Spyridon Louis in a time of 2 hours, 58 minutes and 50 seconds.

Louis was a Greek water-carrier who had never done any competitive running before. He started towards the back, but as more and more runners dropped out he took the lead. When word spread to the stadium that a Greek was leading, the crowd erupted into cheers and by the time Louis reached the stadium two Greek princes were there to accompany him on his final lap. The King of Greece told him he could name his prize, and Louis asked for a cart and donkey to help him in his business.

The first marathons were around 24 to 26 miles, roughly the distance between Marathon and Athens. The first race to be run at the incredibly specific distance of 26 miles and 385 yards was during the 1908 London Olympics. It was extended from the initial 26 miles so that the race would finish in from of the royal box inside the stadium, so that the royal family could observe.

As the race neared its end, the first person into the stadium was Italian runner Donardo Pietre, who had overtaken the leader Charles Hefferon at the 24th mile. He was so tired that he started running the wrong way around the track and had to be turned by race officials. Now completely exhausted he collapsed several times as he finished his lap, and all the while the other contestants were catching up. Finally the clerk and chief medical officer helped him pick himself up, and he still crossed the finish line a full 30 seconds in front of the runner up.

That would not be the end of the matter. Some of the other participants complaint that Pietri received help from officials against the rules, and he was disqualified and the trophy handed to Johnny Hayes of the USA. It was the most controversial event of the Olympics, and the excitement and drama had people talking about it for weeks and cemented the marathon's reputation; as well as ensuring 26.2 miles would become the standard distance.

After those great races, the marathon became a regular Olympic event and races were organized in cities around the world, although the initial competition were only open to male participants. The IAAF considers Violet Piercy the first woman to set a world best in the marathon, when she ran in the

Polytechnic Marathon in London in 1926, despite not having permission or a role as an official participant.

However, it wasn't until 1967 that a woman managed to run with a race number Kathrine Switzer registered for the Boston Marathon as 'KV Swtizer' and officials didn't realize she was a woman until she turned up to compete. There were objections, and race manager Jock Semple even tried to rip off Switzer's race number, which almost led to a punch up between him and Switzer's boyfriend. But finally she was allowed to race, and her finish made headlines around the world.

Things started to change after that, and in 1972 women were welcome in the Boston Marathon. By the 1984 Olympics in Los Angeles it had been decided that a woman's marathon would be held in addition to the men's, the first official female winner of the Olympic marathon was Joan Benoit of the USA, who finished in 2 hours 24 minutes and 52 seconds.

The men's world record is currently held by Dennis Kimetto of Kenya, who ran the Berlin Marathon in 2014 in astonishing 2 hours 2 minutes and 57 seconds. The women's world record is held by Paula Radcliffe of Great Britain, who completed London Marathon in 2003 in an equally impressive 2 hours 15 minutes and 25 seconds.

If you're worried that you're too old to start running marathons, take heart – the world's oldest marathon runner is Fauja Singh, who completed the Toronto Waterfront Marathon in 2011 at the age of 100. Singh didn't even start running until he was 81, when he immigrated to England to live with one of his sons after the death of his wife. He turned up to his first training session in a three-piece suit, but learned quickly and has gone on to run the Hong Kong, New York and London Marathons.

Most of the larger modern marathons are members of the Association of International Marathons and Distance Races (AIMS), which now has more than 400 different distance events in over 100 different countries. The largest of these, part of the World Marathon Majors, are the Berlin, Boston, Chicago, London, New York and Tokyo Marathons. If you run two or more of these races in a single year you are eligible for the WMM prize of $500,000, which goes to the male and female athlete who score the greatest number of points from any two qualifying races.

And if those six major races give you a taste, there are plenty of marathons run in some weird and wonderful places across the planet, The Tromso Midnight Sun Marathon is run in Norway every June. The town of Tromso is within the Arctic Circle and gets 24 hours of light in the middle of summer, so the race begins at 8:30pm so that participants can run in the 'midnight sun'. Even further north, the annual North Pole Marathon involves ten laps around a small loop of ice and snow, run in full winter gear in extremely weather conditions.

You can also choose to race in the Everest Marathon, but beware – it's a 15 day hike to base camp before you even think about running, and then a 15 day hike home. The world's highest marathon takes some acclimatizing to the altitude and thin air, and the hills are steep, but the views can't be beaten. The views are also pretty spectacular on the Great Wall of China Marathon, although the steep and treacherous ascents and descents are not for the faint of heart.

One of the stranger marathons – originally a bet between two friends in a pub – is Llanwrtyd Wells' Man vs Horse Marathon. Although horses are obviously much faster, the mountainous and boggy terrain slows them down and gives the runners a sporting chance. Still, since the race began in 1980 only two men have ever beaten the horses.

The Athens Classic Marathon is staged in modern times along the original route taken by Pheidippides, and is considered one of the toughest marathons in the world with a brutal uphill between 10km and 31km. It passes through hilly terrain and goes past the tomb of the Athenian soldiers who fell in the battle 2,500 years ago before finishing in Panathnaic Stadium, which has been the site of various athletic events since the 6th century BC. The marathon has spread around the world and come full circle, still being run in the place where it all started.

Printed in Great Britain
by Amazon